Looking at
LINCOLN

Fourscore and seven yea

this continent a new nation,

to the proposition that all men a

gaged in a great civil war, testin

so conceived and so dedicated can

battlefield of that war. We have con

as a final resting-place for those

that nation might live. It is altogeth

do this. But in a larger sense, we ca

we cannot hallow this ground. The

struggled here have consecrated

detract. The world will little note

but it can never forget what they

to be dedicated here to the unfini

here have thus far so nobly adva

dedicated to the great task remaini

ored dead we take increased de

they gave the last full measure of d

that these dead shall not hav

under God shall have a new bir

ment of the people, by the peo

perish from the eart

s ago our fathers brought forth on

ceived in **liberty** and dedicated

created equal. Now we are en-

whether that nation or any **nation**

ng endure. We are met on a great

to **dedicate** a portion of that field

ho **here gave their lives** that

r fitting and proper that we should

not dedicate, we cannot consecrate,

rave men, living and dead who

far above our poor power to add or

long remember what we say here,

id here. It is for **us the living** rather

ed **work** which they who fought

ed. It is rather for us to be here

before us—that from **these hon-**

otion to **that cause** for which

otion—that we here highly resolve

died in vain, that **this nation**

of **freedom**, and that govern-

le, for the people shall **not**

—LINCOLN'S GETTYSBURG ADDRESS

Maira Kalman

Looking at LINCOLN

PUFFIN BOOKS

ONE DAY,
WHILE WALKING THROUGH THE PARK
ON MY WAY TO BREAKFAST
I SAW A VERY TALL MAN.
HE REMINDED ME OF SOMEONE,
BUT I COULD NOT THINK WHO.

AT THE COFFEE SHOP I ORDERED PANCAKES.
THEY WERE **DELICIOUS.**

WE PAID WITH A LINCOLN

AND TWO WASHINGTONS.

AND THEN I REMEMBERED.
THE MAN I HAD SEEN LOOKED EXACTLY
LIKE ABRAHAM LINCOLN.

Abraham Lincoln.
The sixteenth president of the United States.

Who was he? I went to the library to find out.
Abraham Lincoln was such an amazing man that
there are over 16,000 books written about him.
I wanted to read them all, but I got lost in
photos of his unusual face.
I stared at one.
I could look at him forever.

He was born in a small log cabin
in Kentucky on February 12, 1809.
The family was poor.
Abe was a dreamer. He did not like to do chores.
He loved to read.

HE WAS LUCKY. HIS STEPMOTHER LOVED him LIKE CRAZY.
AND HE ADORED HER.

SHE LOOKS SO STERN, BUT SHE LET him DREAM
AND READ AS MUCH AS HE WANTED.

Subtraction of Long Mea

L	M	f	P
7	1	3	10
44	2	5	16
21	1	5	34
11	1	3	10

Subr

Y	f	Y	B
48	0	4	2
12	0	3	1
36	0	10	1
48	0	1	2

Of Land Measure

A	R	P	40
12	1	10	
5	3	17	
6	1	33	
12	1	10	

A	R	P	40
17	3	17	
12	3	23	
4	3	34	
17	3	17	

a	r	p	40
28	1	17	
19	1	28	
8	3	19	
28	1	7	

Of Dry Measure

Ch	B	P	36 4
17	2	1	
10	9	3	
7	0	2	
17	2	7	

Cl	Ch	36 4	
40	1	2	
16	5	1	
23	32	1	
30	7	2	

q	B	P	8 4
19	1	1	
12	7	2	
6	1	3	
19	1	1	

Abraham Lincoln
his hand and pen
he will be good but
god knows when

He went to school for only one year.

But he was curious and taught himself many things.

THEY had HARDLY ANY SUPPLIES.
And of course, no electricity.
Abraham spent many hours
reading by the fire's glow.

One day he was kicked in the head by a mule.
He slept for two days.
Then he woke up and grew up
and decided to be a lawyer.

(HE did LiKE To ARGuE.)

He lived in Springfield, Illinois.
And got a reputation as a smart and honest man.
They called him Honest Abe.

He had a family that he loved very much.
His wife, Mary (who was very short), and four sons.
They laughed and had lots of friends and
even ran around a little wild.

I WONDER IF MARY AND ABRAHAM
HAD NICKNAMES FOR EACH OTHER.
DID SHE CALL HIM LINKY?
DID HE CALL HER LITTLE PLUMPY?
MAYBE.

Abe worked hard and
became interested in the government.
He decided he would run for president.
And on March 4, 1861,
he was inaugurated
president of the United States.

ON the DAY HE WAS ELECTED
I BET MARY MADE his FAVORITE VANILLA CAKE.

BUT MAYBE he FORGOT TO EAT his SLICE.
HE WAS OFTEN TOo BUSY Thinking to EAT.

Lincoln wore a very tall hat.
(With his hat on he was seven feet tall.)

He wrote many notes and stuffed them inside his hat.
WHAT WAS he Thinking ABOUT?

He was thinking about democracy.
The Declaration of Independence and the Constitution
created by the founders of this country.

He was thinking
about freedom and
doing good for mankind.

And MAYBE HE WAS ALSO Thinking ABOUT GETTING A BirthdAY PRESENT for his Little Son.

MAYBE A WHISTLE.

OR PICK UP STICKS.

WHAT did he LOVE?

He loved his dog Fido.

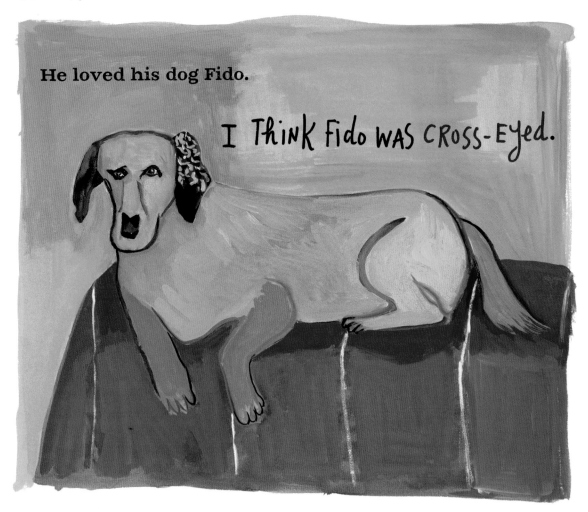

I THINK FIDO WAS CROSS-EYED.

He loved apples.
Cox's orange pippins.
White pippins.
Winesap.
Benoni.

He always had an apple on his desk.

He loved music. He loved Mozart.

ESPECIALLY HIS OPERA
THE MAGIC FLUTE.

But mostly he loved people. His family, of course,
but all people. And he wanted them to live well.
He loved justice and truth.

The country was in trouble
and headed for a war.
After hundreds of years of slavery,
people were saying ENough.

There were courageous people
who fought for liberty,
like Sojourner Truth.

And Frederick Douglass, who had been a slave until he ran away to the North.

Both of them met with Lincoln and spoke of the plight of slaves.

Lincoln **hated** slavery and wrote to a friend,

"If slavery is not wrong, nothing is wrong."

During his presidency
he issued the Emancipation Proclamation,
the first official step
toward freeing millions of slaves.

It was a difficult time to be president.
The Southern states (the Confederacy) wanted
their own country where slavery was allowed.
Lincoln said no. We must stay one country.
The Northern states (the Union) believed
that slavery should be abolished.
And so they went to war.

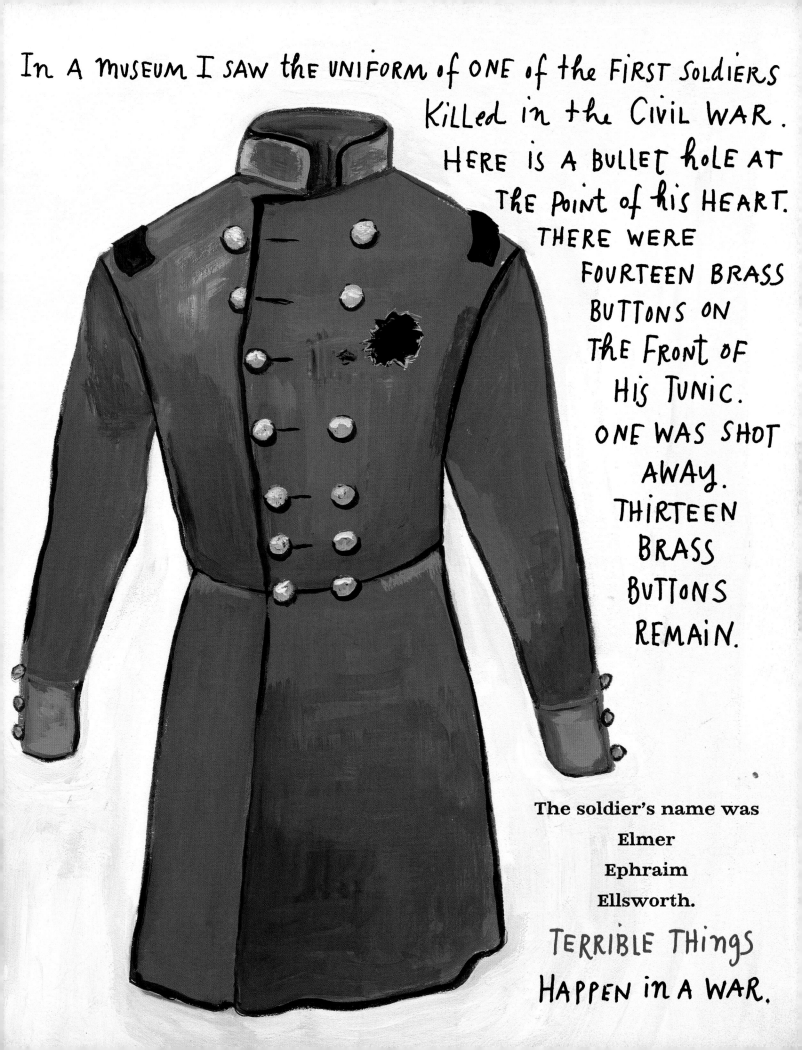

In a museum I saw the uniform of one of the first soldiers killed in the Civil War. Here is a bullet hole at the point of his heart. There were fourteen brass buttons on the front of his tunic. One was shot away. Thirteen brass buttons remain.

The soldier's name was

Elmer

Ephraim

Ellsworth.

Terrible things happen in a war.

The Civil War ground on.

Lincoln went to Gettysburg, Pennsylvania, the site of a big battle.

Thousands of soldiers were buried there.

Many with just a number on their grave.

On that sad land,
Lincoln gave one of history's greatest speeches,
the Gettysburg Address.
It was short—only 272 words—ending with

"... government of the people, by the people,
for the people
shall not perish from the earth."

The war finally ended in 1865. Almost a million people
had been killed or wounded. The North had won.

The people had suffered greatly,
but now it was time to rejoice
and start to rebuild the country
with Lincoln leading the way.

After the agony of the war,

Lincoln wanted to lighten the mood.

He took his wife to see a funny play.

During the play, he was shot.

MURDERED by A WRETChEd MAN
who DiD NOT WANT SLAVERY To END.

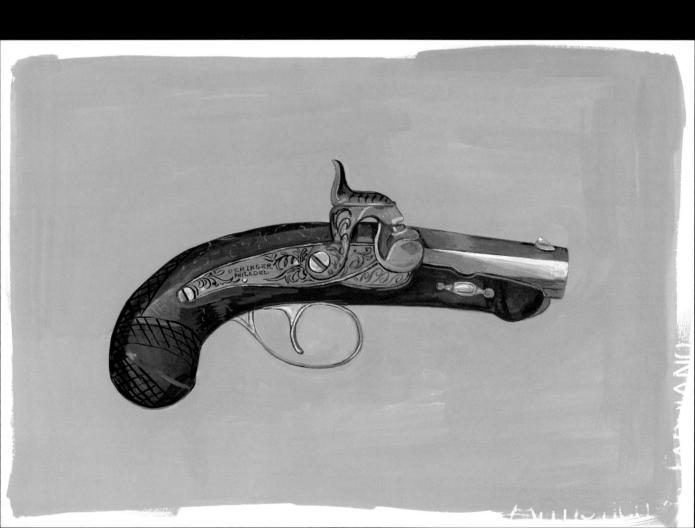

Lincoln had been rocking in this chair.
People carried him across the street
to the home of a friend.
He died the next morning, April 15, 1865.
He was fifty-six years old.

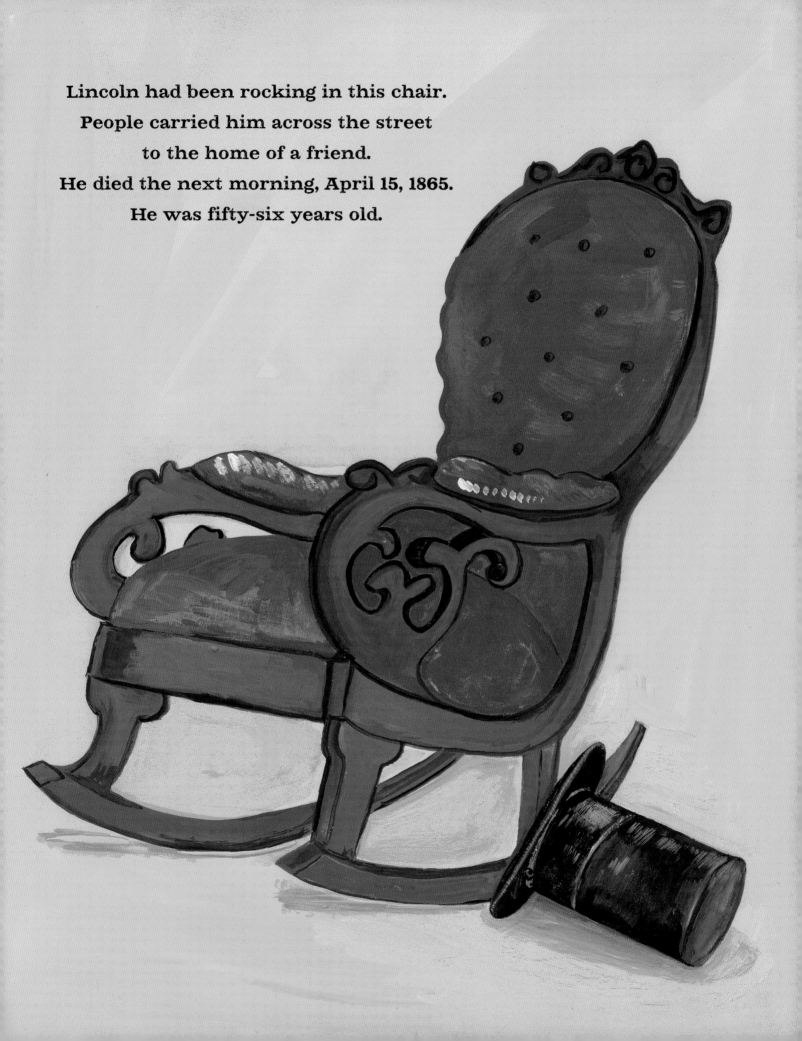

The news spread.
People across the land wept with
grief for their fallen leader.

ABRAHAM LINCOLN
WILL LIVE FOREVER.

And IF YOU GO TO
WASHINGTON, D.C.
in the SPRING
YOU CAN WALK

Through the CHERRY BLOSSOMS AND VISIT him.

AT his MEMORIAL YOU CAN READ THE WORDS
HE WROTE NEAR THE END OF THE WAR.

"... With malice toward none,
with charity for all."

And YOU CAN LOOK into his BEAUTIFUL EYES.
JUST LOOK.

NOTES

LINCOLN PRESENTERS:
Impersonators of the sixteenth president visit schools, libraries and historical societies to bring Lincoln to life. The ideal impersonators are 6 foot 4 inches, just like Lincoln. There is even an Association of Lincoln Presenters, whose motto is "We are ready, willing and ABE L."

LINCOLN'S LOG CABIN:
Lincoln's family migrated west to Illinois, where they built their simple log cabin. The Illinois Historic Preservation Agency operates a site with a reproduction of the cabin.

LINCOLN'S STEPMOTHER:
Abraham Lincoln's mother, Nancy, died in 1818, when he was nine years old. A year later his father, Thomas Lincoln, married Sarah Bush Johnston, a widow with three children. She encouraged Abraham's love of reading, and he was very fond of her and always referred to her as "Mother."

KICKED IN THE HEAD:
In his tenth year, Lincoln was kicked in the head by a horse or a mule (there are varying accounts), and for a brief time he was thought to be dead.

LINCOLN'S CHILDREN:
Lincoln had four sons: Robert Todd, Edward Baker (Eddie), William Wallace (Willie), and Thomas (Tad). Eddie died as a toddler, and Willie died in the White House at age eleven.

LINCOLN'S FAVORITE CAKE:
Mary Todd first baked a vanilla-almond cake for Abraham Lincoln when they were courting. She made it when she was a Springfield housewife and when she was First Lady.

LINCOLN'S DOG:
Fido lived with the Lincoln family in Springfield, Illinois. The mixed-breed dog had to be left behind when the family moved to D.C., as he was terrified of loud noises and Lincoln feared the trip would be too much for him. Some neighbors happily took Fido and his favorite sofa in.

SOJOURNER TRUTH:
Sojourner Truth was a traveling preacher who fought for the abolition of slavery and for women's rights. Her most famous speech was called "Ain't I a Woman?"

FREDERICK DOUGLASS:
Douglass published his autobiography NARRATIVE OF THE LIFE OF FREDERICK DOUGLASS, AN AMERICAN SLAVE, WRITTEN BY HIMSELF to much acclaim and popularity. During the Civil War he fought for the rights of the African American Union Army.

EMANCIPATION PROCLAMATION:
President Abraham Lincoln issued the Emancipation Proclamation on January 1, 1863, during the Civil War. The proclamation declared that "all persons held as slaves" within the rebellious states "shall be then, thenceforward, and forever free."

CIVIL WAR–ERA FLAG:
The flag of the United States during the first half of the Civil War had 34 stars, one for every state of the Union, even those attempting secession. The 33rd star represented Oregon and the 34th Kansas.

CIVIL WAR UNIFORMS:
Early in the war, uniforms were supplied by individual towns and states, so there was a confusing variety. Over time, blue became the color for the North and gray for the Confederate South.

COLONEL ELMER EPHRAIM ELLSWORTH:
Ellsworth was a personal friend of Lincoln's and one of the Union's most promising officers. He was shot in Alexandria, Virginia, in May 1861, after removing a Confederate flag from atop a local inn. His sensational death was the first officer casualty on the front.

GETTYSBURG ADDRESS:
Lincoln's speech, delivered on November 19, 1863, at the Soldiers' National Cemetery in Gettysburg, Pennsylvania, is one of the most famous speeches in United States history.

LINCOLN'S MURDER:
Lincoln was watching a play called OUR AMERICAN COUSIN at Ford's Theatre in Washington, D.C., on April 14, 1865, when he was shot by John Wilkes Booth, actor and Confederate sympathizer. The gun used was a Philadelphia Deringer pistol, on display at the museum in Ford's Theatre.

The chair in which Lincoln was shot is on display at the Henry Ford Museum in Dearborn, Michigan.

LINCOLN'S FUNERAL:
Lincoln was buried in Springfield, Illinois, where he was honored with the military tradition of a riderless horse in his funeral procession. Lincoln's own horse, Old Bob, carried a pair of boots reversed in the stirrups to represent the fallen leader looking back on his troops for the last time.

LINCOLN MEMORIAL:
The nineteen-feet-tall marble statue of Lincoln was built under the supervision of sculptor Daniel Chester French. An inscription above the statue reads: "In this temple, as in the hearts of the people for whom he saved the Union, the memory of Abraham Lincoln is enshrined forever." Martin Luther King Jr. delivered his famous "I Have a Dream" speech from the steps of the Memorial.

SOURCES

Holzer, Harold, ed. ABRAHAM LINCOLN: PORTRAYED IN THE
COLLECTIONS OF THE INDIANA HISTORICAL SOCIETY.
Indianapolis: Indiana Historical Society Press, 2006.

Jennison, Keith W. THE HUMOROUS MR. LINCOLN. New York:
Thomas Y. Crowell Co., 1965.

Junior League of Springfield, Illinois. HONEST TO GOODNESS:
HONESTLY GOOD FOOD FROM MR. LINCOLN'S HOMETOWN.
Nashville: Favorite Recipes Press, 2004.

Kunhardt, Philip B., III; Peter W. Kunhardt; and Peter W.
Kunhardt Jr. LOOKING FOR LINCOLN: THE MAKING OF
AN AMERICAN ICON. New York: Alfred A. Knopf, 2008.

Lorant, Stefan. LINCOLN: A PICTURE STORY OF HIS LIFE.
New York: Bonanza Books, 1979.

McCreary, Donna D. LINCOLN'S TABLE: A PRESIDENT'S CULINARY
JOURNEY FROM CABIN TO COSMOPOLITAN. Charlestown, Ind.:
Lincoln Presentations, 2008.

Mellon, James, ed. THE FACE OF LINCOLN. New York:
Viking Press, 1979.

Meredith, Roy. MR. LINCOLN'S CAMERA MAN: MATHEW B. BRADY.
New York: Charles Scribner's Sons, 1946.

Rubenstein, Harry R. ABRAHAM LINCOLN: AN EXTRAORDINARY LIFE.
Washington, D.C.: Smithsonian Books, 2008.

Sandburg, Carl. ABRAHAM LINCOLN: THE PRAIRIE YEARS AND
THE WAR YEARS. New York: Harcourt, Brace and Co., 1954.

Schwartz, Thomas F. MARY TODD LINCOLN: FIRST LADY
OF CONTROVERSY. Springfield, Ill.: Abraham Lincoln
Presidential Library Foundation, 2007.

Wills, Chuck. LINCOLN: THE PRESIDENTIAL ARCHIVES.
New York: DK Publishing, 2007.

Wilson, Douglas L. HONOR'S VOICE: THE TRANSFORMATION
OF ABRAHAM LINCOLN. New York: Alfred A. Knopf, 1998.

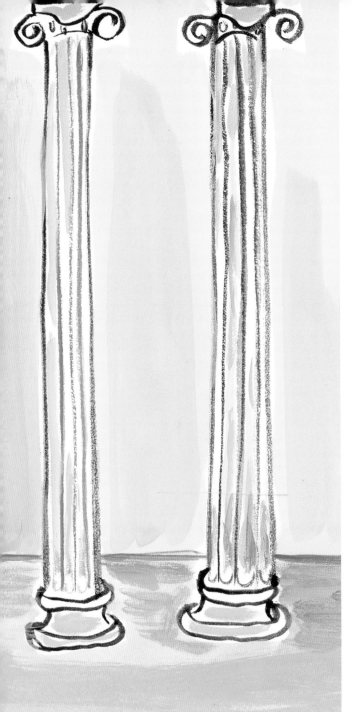

This one is for Abe

and

for Lulu and Alex

PUFFIN BOOKS
An imprint of Penguin Random House LLC
375 Hudson Street
New York, New York 10014

First published in the United States of America
by Nancy Paulsen Books,
a division of Penguin Young Readers Group, 2012
Published by Puffin Books, an imprint of
Penguin Random House LLC, 2017

THE LIBRARY OF CONGRESS HAS CATALOGED THE
NANCY PAULSEN BOOKS EDITION AS FOLLOWS:
Kalman, Maira.
Looking at Lincoln / Maira Kalman.
Summary: A brief look at the life of United States president
Abraham Lincoln.
ISBN 9780399240393 (hardcover)
[1. Lincoln, Abraham, 1809–1865—Juvenile literature.
2. Lincoln, Abraham, 1809–1865. 3. Presidents—
United States—Biography—Juvenile literature. 4. United
States—History—Civil War, 1861–1865—Juvenile literature.
5. United States—History—Civil War, 1861–1865.]
E457.905 .K26 2012

Puffin Books ISBN 9780147517982

Manufactured in China

1 3 5 7 9 10 8 6 4 2

Design by Marikka Tamura

The art was done in gouache.

PRAISE FOR *THOMAS JEFFERSON*

★ "Conveys clearly [Jefferson's] contribution to the growing nation as founding father and president . . . Impressive complexity put artfully and respectfully within the grasps of young readers."
——*Kirkus Reviews*, starred review

★ "The inimitable Kalman brings her wit, wisdom, and beautifully unique artwork to one of America's most complex founding fathers: Thomas Jefferson . . . Share this along with the author's picture-book biography of Abraham Lincoln, *Looking at Lincoln*, to inspire young historians and artists alike."
——*School Library Journal*, starred review

★ "The voice is that of a curious child reporting fascinating research findings . . . Playful but informative, as quick witted as Jefferson himself, this will inspire young readers to learn more."
——*Booklist*, starred review

"Kalman dwells in conflict and raises questions to the end, pronouncing Monticello a symbol of all that is 'optimistic and complex and tragic and wrong and courageous' about America."
——*Publishers Weekly*

PRAISE FOR *NEXT STOP GRAND CENTRAL*

★ "From cover to cover, this is a giddy, quirky, unforgettable romp through 'the busiest, fastest, biggest place there is,' the truly grand Grand Central Station. All aboard!" ——*School Library Journal*, starred review

"All the familiar and eccentric sorts are represented, with great originality and in brilliant color."
——*The New York Times Book Review*

"Kalman succeeds in recreating the station's frenetic pace and the blurred sense of passersby, and her creative reportage conveys the importance of all the individuals whose lives intersect at New York's Grand Central Terminal." ——*Publishers Weekly*

"Grand Central is a grand adventure—and Kalman's book is a first-class ticket to ride."
——*The Horn Book Magazine*

"The paintings are vivacious as ever and truly capture the building's grandeur and eclecticism."
——*Kirkus Reviews*

PRAISE FOR *FIREBOAT*

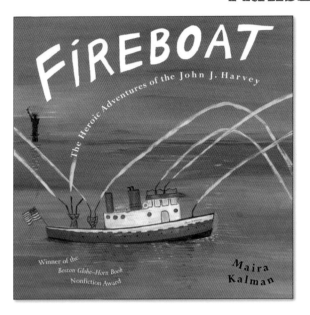

★ "Kalman does some extraordinary things in this beautiful picture book . . . Her artistry is as compassionate as it is brilliant . . . A hundred years from now, when people want to know what we told our children about 9/11, Kalman's book should be among the first answers."
—*Booklist*, starred review

★ "*Fireboat* does many things. It sets forth an adventure, helps commemorate an anniversary, offers an interesting bit of history, celebrates the underdog, and honors the fire-fighting profession. Children and adults will respond to it in as many ways."
—*School Library Journal*, starred review

★ "Kalman intelligently conveys those unfathomable events in a way that a picture book audience can comprehend . . . With this inspiring book, Kalman sensitively handles a difficult subject in an age-appropriate manner."
—*Publishers Weekly*, starred review

★ "Among the many literary tributes to 9-11 heroism, Kalman's is particularly exciting, uplifting, and child-sensitive . . . Revisits the tragedy without the terror and conveys pride without preachiness."
—*The Bulletin of the Center for Children's Books*, starred review

★ "Quintessential New York artist Kalman gives us an idiosyncratic but informative look at a Big Apple institution . . . Kalman's use of the events of September 11 is honest and honorable, and rarely is she as straightforward as she is here."
—*The Horn Book*, starred review

PRAISE FOR *WHAT PETE ATE FROM A–Z*

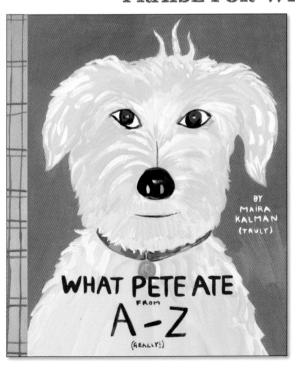

"Kalman paints affectionate portraits of the unstoppable Pete . . . and her hand-printed text acts as an element of the illustrations. Her overblown alliteration and fabulous gouaches gush with glamour."
—*Publishers Weekly*

"Kalman presents her own distinctly different, slyly funny ABC . . . Such word-y adventures find a pictorial match in Kalman's pseudo-primitive gouache illustrations."
—*Children's Literature*

"The paintings carry Kalman's signature zany energy, with Pete, a blond, bearded mutt, frequently portrayed with the remains of his unconventional diet hanging out of his mouth."
—*Kirkus Reviews*